GRUNGIER JOKES

GRUNGIER JOKES

SEATTLE SAL

S.P.I. BOOKS
A Division Of Shapolsky Publishers

Grungier Jokes

S.P.I. BOOKS
A division of Shapolsky Publishers, Inc.

ISBN 1-56171-262-0

For any additional information, contact:

S.P.I. BOOKS/Shapolsky Publishers, Inc.
136 West 22nd Street
New York, NY 10011
212/633-2022 / FAX 212/633-2123

Manufactured in Canada

10 9 8 7 6 5 4 3 2 1

CONTENTS

DEDICATION

To My Parents...
Sorry, Mom
You too, Dad, even though you
called the cops on me.

CHAPTER ONE

MUSICALLY SPEAKING

What's the difference between Madonna and a shark?

☞ When a man is eaten by a shark, he's better off!

☹ ☹ ☹

What's the difference between Madonna and a wolf?

☞ The lip gloss and the pointy bras.

☹ ☹ ☹

What do you call a guy who can't score with Madonna, Cher or Shannon Doherty?

☞ A Certifiable Gay.

☹ ☹ ☹

What's the difference between Prince and Madonna?

☞ Madonna uses less mascara.

☹ ☹ ☹

What's Madonna's favorite bird?

☞ A woodpecker.

☹ ☹ ☹

What's dinner for four for Madonna?

☞ 69 twice.

☹ ☹ ☹

Why does Madonna like going down on young boys?

☞ Less filling, tastes great.

☹ ☹ ☹

What is Madonna's vagina to her lovers?

☞ A window into her soul.

☹ ☹ ☹

Why is Madonna so much like a chicken farmer?

☞ They both make their living raising cocks.
(Madonna also inspires girls to raise their dresses).

☹ ☹ ☹

Why does Madonna like masturbation so much?

☞ Because it's sex with someone she really loves.

☹ ☹ ☹

How can you tell if Madonna is formally dressed?

☞ If those flapping tits are in her shirt.

☹ ☹ ☹

Why does Madonna insist her guys slap her around before sex?

☞ She likes her men to Rock 'n' Roll her.

☹ ☹ ☹

Why does Madonna always wear sleeveless shirts?

☞ Because she's into armpit intercourse.

☹ ☹ ☹

Why are Madonna and Shannon Doherty like apes?

☞ Because those two publicity seeking sluts are born to be wild.

☹ ☹ ☹

What is Shannon Doherty's favorite vacation spot?

☞ Down Under.

☹ ☹ ☹

Why does Shannon Doherty keep getting arrested while living her wild L.A. lifestyle?

☞ Because she loves penal institutions.

☹ ☹ ☹

Why does Shannon Doherty always wear tight pants?

☞ To keep her brains from leaking out.

☹ ☹ ☹

What is the proper way to characterize a marriage between Shannon Doherty and a gorilla?

☞ Social climbing.

☹ ☹ ☹

What's Hard Rock to a nerd?

☞ Barry Manilow singing the best of Neil Diamond.

☹ ☹ ☹

Why do Rock 'n' Roll fans always wear black?

☞ They're mourning over the death of music.

☹ ☹ ☹

What's the main use for Punk Rock music in Attica?

☞ It's what a lifer uses to threaten a new prisoner into taking it up the ass.

☹ ☹ ☹

What do you find in a New Wave Japanese garden?

☞ Punk rocks.

☹ ☹ ☹

What's the difference between George Steinbrenner and Bruce Springsteen?

☞ Both are Bosses, but only one's an asshole.

☹ ☹ ☹

What was the difference between Elvis's wedding and his funeral?

☞ About 300 pounds.

☹ ☹ ☹

How do we know Elvis was a huge star?

☞ He had to be buried in a piano case.

☹ ☹ ☹

What do you call an all-girl rock band that gives blow jobs?

☞ A headband.

☹ ☹ ☹

Why are so many rock musicians like warped records?

☞ They end up stuck on needles.

☹ ☹ ☹

Did you hear the one about Beethoven's 9th Symphony?

☞ Neither did he.

CHAPTER TWO

BILL-IOUS AND HILLARY-OUS: THE CLINTON FAMILY JOKES

What's safe sex for Bill Clinton?

☞ Anytime Hillary's out of town.

☹ ☹ ☹

How did President Clinton meet Hillary?

☞ They were both fucking the same girl while in college.

☹ ☹ ☹

What would you get if you crossed a Ted Kennedy with a Billy Carter?

☞ A Bill Clinton.

☹ ☹ ☹

What was Bill Clinton's college weight-loss program?

☞ Running....from the draft.

☹ ☹ ☹

Why did the hot-looking, sweet, young sexy musician fuck Bill Clinton?

☞ He had lots of sax appeal.

☹ ☹ ☹

Why can't you shit if you voted with Ross Perot against NAFTA?

☞ Because your fuckin asshole is over in Texas.

☹ ☹ ☹

What was Fleetwood Mac's employment advice to Bill?

☞ "Start Thinking About Tomorrow."

☹ ☹ ☹

What do you get when you cross Bill Clinton and a breakfast?

☞ President McMuffin.

☹ ☹ ☹

What do you get when you cross Bill Clinton and a roll?

☞ The Billsbury Doughboy.

☹ ☹ ☹

What chicken parts has Bill Clinton been favoring since he was elected?

☞ Right wings and assholes.

☹ ☹ ☹

What do you call a Razorback with half a brain?

☞ Mr. President.

"BILL'S FAVES":

Favorite Color:	Pinko
Favorite Car:	Pickup Truck
Favorite Philosopher:	Timothy Leary
Favorite TV program:	Beverly Hillbillies (obviously)
Favorite Singer:	Tammy Wynette (Also Hillary's favorite, as we all know from her comments during Bill's election campaign).
Favorite Book:	The T-Factor Fat Gram Counter
Favorite Song:	Why's Everyone Always Picking On Me?
Favorite Sport:	Lunch and dinner
Favorite Recliner:	La-Z-Boy
Favorite Babe:	Elly May Clampett (and any piece of ass that knows how to spread her thighs and keep her mouth shut)

TOP TEN WAYS BILL CAN DROP EVEN LOWER IN THE POLLS

10. Dump Hillary for a real woman like Cindy Crawford or Michelle Pfeiffer
9. Jog shirtless
8. Pardon Joey Buttafuocco
7. Tell Mother Theresa to "Kiss my white ass"
6. Reveal that he once traveled with Jane Fonda to Hanoi
5. Guest star on "Murphy Brown" and impregnate Candice Bergen (on camera)
4. Drown that useless pet Socks in the Potomac
3. Appoint Arnold Schwarzenegger Ambassador to Israel
2. Admit he has "lust in his heart", ... for Rush Limbaugh
1. Replace Gore

"REVISIONISM: HILLARY BEFORE AND AFTER THE ELECTION":

Old Description Of The Bitch	New Description Of The First Lady
Heavy-handed	Politically-savvy
Meddler	Policy insider
Ideologue	Advocate
Over-achiever	Terribly competent
Social climbing	Washington wife
Left-of-center	Mainstream
Too ambitious	Career-minded
Corporate animal	Home maker
Serious	Good-humored
Opportunistic	Astute
Ugly	Trendy lady
Cunning	Practical
Domineering	Influential
Lesbian Dyke	Ideal wife
Radical	Role-model
Fashion nerd	Trend-setter
Mean bitch	Obedient
Aloof	Well-behaved
Wears the pants	Subdued

"TOP 10 REASONS WHY HILLARY SHOULD BE THANKFUL TO GENNIFER":

10. Once-in-a-lifetime opportunity to appear on *60 Minutes*.

9. A great excuse to spend big bucks on a new wardrobe and hairdo.

8. Turned out the Gary Hart sympathy vote for Bill.

7. Earned the admiration of millions of American who always thought Tammy Wynette was a whining little bitch.

6. Proved once and for all Bill's uncanny resemblance to JFK.

5. Helped create the losing family-values theme for Republican convention.

4. Even made Bob Dole feel sorry for her.

3. Took publicity spotlight off Socks the dumb cat.

2. Convinced Bill to be much more discreet the next time.

1. Saved the family big bucks in blackmail payments to that publicity-seeking whore slut-bag.

☹ ☹ ☹

If Bill Clinton and Hillary Clinton were stranded on a sinking cruise ship, who would be rescued?

☞ The American people.

☹ ☹ ☹

What was the worst mistake Senator Bob Packwood made with his infamous secret diaries?

☞ Not letting Ted Kennedy and William Kennedy Smith handle his damage control.

CHAPTER THREE

AND WHY ARE THE DUMB-SHIT REPUBLICAN LOSERS LAUGHING?

What's the Republican position on the danger to our country from acid rain?

☞ Building a sky dome to cover the Rose Garden whenever it clouds up. (Fuck those idiots in the middle class).

☹ ☹ ☹

What's the only kind of class oppression the Republicans will do something about?

☞ Teachers who won't let their school kids out for recess. (Fuck those liberal teacher bitches).

☹ ☹ ☹

What's the Republican solution to the problem of expanding nuclear waste?

☞ Sit ups. (Fuck those idiot American voters).

☹ ☹ ☹

According to Republicans, what's the major Hispanic social problem in America?

☞ The growing Chevy shortage. (Fuck those idiots in the lower classes—those lazy immigrant bastards).

☹ ☹ ☹

What's a feminist Republican's main position?

☞ Women should have the right to vote just like their husbands. (That's the way to train our obedient Republican bitches!).

☹ ☹ ☹

What's the Republican attitude toward blacks?

☞ They look swell dressed up on lawns. (Fuck those welfare cheating bastards—they don't vote anyway).

☹ ☹ ☹

What's the Republican position on Imperialism?

☞ Chrysler doesn't make the car it once did. (Fuck those other countries—we don't need those Third World losers and they don't vote anyway).

☹ ☹ ☹

What's the Republican position on Beavis and Butt-Head?

☞ They represent the values and future of the Democratic Party. (Fuck those Liberal Democrats and all the damage they've done to our culture by insisting free speech is necessary. Now they can have their own troubles with their Beavis and Butt-Head-imitating, scum-bag, useless kids!)

☹ ☹ ☹

What do you call people who write ad copy and speeches for Republican campaigns?

☞ Joke writers. (Fuck whoever came up with this question you jerk-off, anti-Republican Seattle Sal piece of shit. Fuck you and your whole un-Republican, unproductive race and generation of losers!)

☹ ☹ ☹

Why is the elephant the symbol of the Republican Party?

☞ Because they have the undisputed, biggest assholes. (Fuck the person who created this joke: Fuck the author Seattle Sal, Fuck the Publisher S.P.I. Books and Fuck anyone who actually thinks this is funny, you silly little bastards!)

☹ ☹ ☹

He may not call himself a Republican, but...What is that giant sucking noise Ross Perot keeps talking about in reference to jobs being lost to Mexico?

1) His ears flapping and creating a backdraft.

2) His sucking up to the average American "little guy" that he *really* supposedly gives a shit about.

3) The blow job he gets after the snow job he gives.

4) His laughter about people who actually believe his line of bullshit.

CHAPTER FOUR

CROSS-CULTURAL CUT-UPS

What's it called when a Californian burns up in a brush fire during an earthquake?

☞ Shake'n Bake.

☹ ☹ ☹

How many Californians does it take to screw in a light bulb?

☞ None. Californians don't screw in light bulbs. They screw in hot tubs.

☹ ☹ ☹

Why are preppie women such lousy lovers?

☞ They're all mannequin depressives. (Seattle Sal would like to remind you that they're also cold, calculating cunts.)

☹ ☹ ☹

A rich preppie man is trying to appease his unhappy wife:

"I'll buy you a Cuisinart," he promises.

She shakes her head no.

"A mink?"

"No."

"A trip to Europe?"

"No."

"How about a Jaguar?" he asks.

"No."

"A new house?"

Still "No." Her resolve is adamant.

"Well, what is it you want?"

"A divorce," she tells him.

"Fuck you! I wasn't planning to spend that much!"

☹ ☹ ☹

Why are so many rich preppie women anorexic?

1) To be more down to earth and identify with the world's starving people.

2) To fit on couches with their fat cat husbands.

3) Sharp body edges are better to repel sex.

☹ ☹ ☹

A college student from the sticks asked his preppie roommate: "Who you going to the dance with?"

The preppie replied: "Don't you know that you don't end a sentence with a preposition."

"Okay," the disgusted student replied, "Who are you going to the dance with, asshole?"

☹ ☹ ☹

Why do yuppies consider sex counterproductive?

☞ You have to start at the top and work to the bottom.

☹ ☹ ☹

What's an unforgettable sexual experience for a yuppie?

☞ Orgasms on the first and fifteenth of the month.

☹ ☹ ☹

What's a yuppie in Arkansas?

☞ A shoe clerk with a charge card at K-Mart.

☹ ☹ ☹

How do we know *Playboy* magazine is going yuppie?

☞ Their last centerfold was a Saab with its hatch wide open.

☹ ☹ ☹

Did you hear about the promiscuous gay sailor?

☞ He left no stern unturned.

☹ ☹ ☹

What's black and white and red all over?

☞ A white woman fucking a black man while she has her period.

☹ ☹ ☹

What's the favorite saying in gay bars?

☞ Do you want me to push in your stool?

☹ ☹ ☹

A gay guy went to a doctor complaining of rectal pain. The doctor examines him and says, "For God's sake, they're two dozen roses up your ass."

All excited, the gay says, "Read the card! Read the card!"

☹ ☹ ☹

What's the difference between a Jewish mother and a vulture?

☞ The vulture waits until you're dead before eating your heart out.

☹ ☹ ☹

What do you call it when a redneck butt-screws a pig?

☞ An old-fashioned couple.

☹ ☹ ☹

How did the redneck who was married to his cousin discover his wife was definitely cheating on him?

☞ She gave birth to a baby with a normal shaped head.

☹ ☹ ☹

Redneck plumbers do it up the waste line.

☹ ☹ ☹

What did the smitten redneck sing to the good-looking pig?

☞ "You Are My Bunshine."

☹ ☹ ☹

What do you call a redneck girl who hasn't been raped by her father, brothers, or cousins?

☞ Runaway.

☹ ☹ ☹

How many Texans does it take to eat an armadillo?

☞ Two: one to eat it and one to watch for oncoming cars.

☹ ☹ ☹

What's the difference between a hippie and an infant?

☞ Infants eventually grow up.

☹ ☹ ☹

How do we know the Sixties generation is hopelessly naive?

☞ These assholes actually believe they made the world a better place.

☹ ☹ ☹

What's the definition of a Sixties radical?

☞ A toxic waste.

☹ ☹ ☹

SEATTLE SAL'S "GUESS THE CULTURAL GROUP GAME":

(When you're not sure of the correct answer, it's acceptable to name the preferred cultural group that you hate.)

☹ ☹ ☹

Two men are walking by an organ grinder. One gives the monkey a dollar. The other says, "I thought you didn't like ________s."

☞ Suggested answers:

A. Blacks

B. Puerto Ricans

C. Midgets

The other man replies: "But the little ________s are so cute when they're that young."

☞ Suggested answers:

A. Scum bags

B. Black bastards

C. Coons

D. Dirt bags

☹ ☹ ☹

What is virgin wool?

☞ Wool from sheep from any country but ____________.

A. Italy

B. Poland

C. Greece

☹ ☹ ☹

What did the Minister say at the__________wedding?

☞ I now pronounce you man and sheep.

A. Australian

B. Arab

C. Red neck

D. White trash

☹ ☹ ☹

What's fun in bed for a ______?

☞ Playing dead.

A. Abused Jewish husband

B. Busy hooker

C. Tired nympho slut

☹ ☹ ☹

What's the easiest way to bump off a ________?

☞ Slam the toilet seat on his head while he's quenching his thirst?

A. Arab

B. Dominican

C. Homeless person

☹ ☹ ☹

How do ________ hold their liquor? (Licker)

☞ By the ears.

A. He men

B. Women haters

C. Jocks

D. Jerks

☹ ☹ ☹

What do you call a ______ with five rats?

☞ A rancher.

A. Libyan

B. Syrian

C. Palestinian

D. Iraqi

☹ ☹ ☹

What happens when a ______doesn't pay his garbage bill?

☞ They stop delivering.

A. Pollack

B. Spick

C. Black

D. Welfare cheat

☹ ☹ ☹

How do you get three _____off a couch?

☞ Jerk one off and the other two will come.

A. Fags

B. Frigid bitches

C. Tough jocks

D. Dykes

☹ ☹ ☹

What's shit on the curb for a _______?

☞ Sidewalk art.

A. Beavis and Butt-Head

B. Politician

C. Homo

D. Dog

☹ ☹ ☹

What do you call a ________ who can write his/her name?

☞ Author.

A. Black man
B. Robber/mugger
C. Pro ball player
D. Cheerleader

☹ ☹ ☹

What do you call Mike Tyson as long as he's in jail?

☞ Answer: ________

A. Boy
B. Coon
C. Dumb shit
D. Moolanyam (Italian term)

E. Rapist motherfucker

F. Shvartzah (Yiddish term)

☹ ☹ ☹

What do you call Mike Tyson when he gets out of jail?

A. Sir

B. Mister

C. My esteemed colleague

D. Master Tyson

☹ ☹ ☹

Why can't you circumcise________?

☞ There's no end to those pricks.

A. Iraqis

B. Beavis and Butt-Head

C. Politicians

D. Lawyers

E. Accountants

F. Euro-trash

G. Snoopy parents

CHAPTER FIVE

GRUNGE GOES INTERNATIONAL

What's full disclosure in the Russian press?

☞ Yeltsin photographed in a bathing suit.

☹ ☹ ☹

How can Russians so easily tolerate waiting on endless lines for toilet paper?

☞ They're so used to being shit on.

☹ ☹ ☹

What will be one of the most unusual developments resulting from the North American Free Trade Agreement (NAFTA)?

☞ American busboys in Mexico's restaurants.

☹ ☹ ☹

What do the Russian and American governments have in common?

☞ Liars and cheats in high places.

☹ ☹ ☹

WOMEN WHO CAN SAY NO!

What do you call a Russian woman who won't make love to her husband?

☞ A Refusnik.

What do you call an Iraqi woman who won't make love to her husband?

☞ Discriminating—but also dead.

What do you call a Puerto Rican woman who won't make love to her husband?

☞ Pregnant again.

What do you call an American woman who wont make love to her husband?

☞ A Bitch!

What do you call a Black woman who won't make love to her husband?

☞ A dead bitch.

What do you call a Mafioso's woman who wont make love to her husband?

☞ A missing bitch.

What do you call an Ivy Leaguer's woman who won't make love to her husband?

☞ A spoiled, preppy, cunning bitch.

What do you call Beavis and Butt-Heads' women that won't sleep with them?

☞ Blind and deaf—What other explanation could there be for them to be with those two losers in the first place.

☹ ☹ ☹

What's a Russian's idea of a fancy dessert?

☞ Frozen tundra.

☹ ☹ ☹

What's Jeffrey Dahmer's idea of a fancy dessert?

☞ A nice piece of ass.

☹ ☹ ☹

What's a Somali's idea of a fancy dessert?

☞ A cup of water.

☹ ☹ ☹

What did the Russian wife call her sexually inadequate husband?

☞ Ivan the Terrible.

☹ ☹ ☹

What does a Russian boxer have in common with a Catskill comedian?

☞ They're both Borscht belters.

☹ ☹ ☹

Overheard in a Greek barber shop:

☞ "You still you using that greasy kid?"

☹ ☹ ☹

What did the constipated Mexican say to his complaining wife?

☞ "The end justifies the beans."

☹ ☹ ☹

What's a six-pack and a potato referred to in Ireland?

☞ An Irish seven course meal.

☹ ☹ ☹

What's long and green with an IQ of 40?

☞ The St. Patrick's Day Parade.

☹ ☹ ☹

How did they resolve the St. Patrick's Day Parade controversy over the admission of Gays in the parade?

☞ Both sides compromised: Only gay priests would march.

☹ ☹ ☹

Then there was the Polack who took a drive in the country to go hunting for big game. When he came to a sign that said "bear left", he went home.

☹ ☹ ☹

What do the Irish the lawn call chairs that they use on their patios?

☞ Patty O'Furniture.

☹ ☹ ☹

Did you hear about the two gay Irishmen?

☞ Gerald Fitszmichael and Michael Fitszgerald.

☹ ☹ ☹

What's the first line of the Puerto Rican National Anthem?

☞ "I'll take Manhattan, The Bronx, and Staten Island ..."

☹ ☹ ☹

What do you call a prostitute from Holland?

☞ A Dutch Oven.

☹ ☹ ☹

During the early days of World War II an international reconnaissance team was sent behind German lines. Made up of a Brit, a Frenchie and a Pole, they moved silently through the Black Forest in search of a secret rocket factory. Suddenly, they all heard German voices

"A patrol," the Brit warned his comrades.

"Mon Dieu," whispered the Frenchie, "what do we do?"

"Quick," said the Brit team leader, "climb trees. Hide in the foliage. Keep absolutely silent."

Up they went, just as the German patrol passed under the trees they'd climbed.

As the Germans moved beneath a large pine, the Brit lost his footing, shaking a branch.

"Vat was dat?" shouted a Wehrmacht Officer.

The Brit thought quickly. He had one chance and only one. "Caw, caw," he called out. "Caw, Caw."

The German shook his head. "Ach, it is just a bird."

The patrol moved on underneath the Frenchie's tree and he too lost his footing, rustling the branches.

"Vait!" called the German.

Thinking quickly, the Frenchman imitated his British ally. "Coo, coo," he sang out.

Satisfied, again the Germans moved on, until they were underneath the Pole's tree. And wouldn't you know it, the Pole's foot slipped too, rustling some branches.

"Halten!" erupted the Nazi patrol leader.

The Pole thought quickly, and following his comrades-in-arms, he convincingly sang out, "Mooooo!, Moooooo!"

☹ ☹ ☹

Did you hear about the Afrikaner geologist?

☞ He was a Boring asshole. (For dumbshit readers who don't get this joke, the Boers are one of the ethnic groups in South Africa. If you understand this, then the joke makes sense. Otherwise, you'll never understand the joke which means you are an illiterate fuck too stupid to continue reading my jokes. Go back to watching Beavis and Butt-Head and get the fuck away from me.
Thank you, Seattle Sal).

☹ ☹ ☹

Then there was the racist South African who declared he'd rather die than be buried in a black cemetery.

☹ ☹ ☹

What's the difference between an Afrikaner and an ostrich?

☞ When the Afrikaner's head isn't in the sand it's up his ass.

☹ ☹ ☹

Three Greatest Japanese Lies:

☞ America gleat country.

☞ What trade barriers?

☞ We've forgotten all bout the war.

☹ ☹ ☹

Did you hear about the new Israeli game show?

☞ *Blame that Arab.*

☹ ☹ ☹

What do you call a convicted thief in Iran?

☞ Lefty.

☹ ☹ ☹

What's a two-time convicted thief called in Iran?

☞ Stumpy.

☹ ☹ ☹

And what's a three-time convicted thief called in Iran?

☞ A parapalegic.

MID-EAST MADNESS:

THOSE CRAZY DIAPER HEADS AND PANTY HEADS!

☹ ☹ ☹

How did Iraqi soldiers make love during Operation Desert Storm?

☞ U.S. Army statistics claim: Left handed.

☹ ☹ ☹

Why is it dangerous to buy drugs from Iraqis?

☞ Because they don't know their Hash From A Hole In The Ground.

☹ ☹ ☹

What do you call horny Arabs?

☞ Camel-holics.

☹ ☹ ☹

What is the Israeli Army's most important training film?

☞ *Lifestyles of The Rich And Famous.*

☹ ☹ ☹

What is the most popular Army Recruiting Poster in the Arab world?

☞ "Join The Army....And See The Next World"

☹ ☹ ☹

What is the proper Mid-Eastern term to refer to someone with rats in their tent?

☞ Rancher.

☹ ☹ ☹

What does L.A. Madam Heidi Fleiss have in common with Israeli leader Yitzak Rabin?

☞ Both are into serious piece negotiations.

☹ ☹ ☹

What do you call Arabs who order Perrier and water?

☞ Sophisticated.

CHAPTER SIX

PICKING ON PROFESSIONALS

What do whores and lawyers have in common?

☞ They'll both suck you dry for a price.

☹ ☹ ☹

How are honest lawyers like nuclear safety?

☞ Neither exists.

☹ ☹ ☹

What's a synonym for lawyer?

☞ Hypocrite (or scumbag).

☹ ☹ ☹

What's ABA stand for?

☞ American Bloodsuckers Association (or for you dumbshits, it really means the American Bar Association. Now do you get this joke? I hate having to explain my jokes to you ignorant fucks who are too stupid to understand them. Pick up a fuckin newspaper, educate your dumb self, and then continue reading my very funny book. Thank you, Seattle Sal).

☹ ☹ ☹

What's the difference between a lawyer and a vulture?

☞ Lawyers' wing tips come off.

☹ ☹ ☹

What do the ABA and the AMA have in common?

☞ Assholes and thieves by the millions.

☹ ☹ ☹

Why do Mafia lawyers make good financial sense?

☞ They're reusable scumbags.

☹ ☹ ☹

What's the difference between a hog and a Mob lawyer?

☞ Hogs wallow for free.

☹ ☹ ☹

What do you call an attorney who describes himself as a criminal lawyer?

☞ Self-aware.

(Let me ask you something, readers. Don't we all agree that lawyers are a bunch of conniving motherfuckers? Am I right on with this observation? Well if you agree, please send me your best Lawyer Jokes and I'll put em in my next book. Also, I'll put your name in the book as a thank you for the good jokes that we actually use.

And as a reward, I'll send you a copy of my last book GRUNGE JOKES ($4.99 retail price) for free! The only catch is that I've got to ask you to send in $3.00 for shipping and handling. The address to send your suggested jokes, your money and your address to receive your complimentary book is:

S.P.I. Books
136 West 22nd St.
New York, NY 10011

You can send check, money order or cash made out to S.P.I. Books).

☹ ☹ ☹

What do you get when you combine a dog and a lawyer?

☞ A legal beagle.

☹ ☹ ☹

When you combine a cheetah and a lawyer, what do you end up with?

☞ The world's best ambulance chaser.

☹ ☹ ☹

What do chilled artichokes and doctors have in common?

☞ Small, cold hearts. (Readers, ain't this the truth. Fuck all the Doctors, too. They're worse than the lawyers – if that's at all possible. The same offer goes to you any for any Doctors Jokes . Send em to me for my next book. You know what you'll get back from me. See the details indicated 2 pages ago for the Lawyer Jokes. I'll send you a free book for your Jokes!).

☹ ☹ ☹

What do you call a Mafia lawyer's office?

☞ A pig sty.

☹ ☹ ☹

Did you hear about the modest doctor?

☞ Me neither. (Please send me more Doctor Jokes. I really hate those pricks!)

☹ ☹ ☹

What are Doctors' favorite letter?

☞ I. (Those greedy, money-oriented, rat-bastards).

☹ ☹ ☹

Did you hear about the gynecologist who went broke?

☞ He was afraid of the dark. (He was also afraid of tunnels!)

☹ ☹ ☹

Why is a proctologist just like a foreman in a furniture factory?

☞ They both inspect stools.

☹ ☹ ☹

What do Doctors have in common with Shannon Doherty?

☞ Both think they're better than you are.

☹ ☹ ☹

What's are fashion models' favorite book?

☞ *No Thighs in Thirty Days.* (Also popular is: *How To Keep Your Thighs Closed*)

☹ ☹ ☹

What do you get when you combine a model and an elephant?

☞ "Dumbo the Retarded. "

☹ ☹ ☹

How can you identify a fashion model?

☞ She's the stick with no tits, personality or brains who's wearing the Channel Jewelry.

☹ ☹ ☹

Why are male models such pricks?

☞ Because you are what you eat.

☹ ☹ ☹

Why are male models frequent prison visitors?

☞ Penal envy.

☹ ☹ ☹

What's walking and chewing gum to a model?

☞ A challenge.

☹ ☹ ☹

What's it like trying to have a intelligent conversation with a model?

☞ It's like trying to have an intelligent conversation with Beavis and Butt-Head.

☹ ☹ ☹

Why did the actress suck down her steak without chewing?

☞ Old habits are hard to break.

☹ ☹ ☹

Hollywood's a place where they shoot too many films.... and not enough actors.

☹ ☹ ☹

Then there's the Hollywood version of the eternal final triangle:
An actor, his wife, and himself.

☹ ☹ ☹

What's the difference between a starlet and a harlot?

☞ A harlot doesn't have to get up early?

☹ ☹ ☹

What do you get when you combine an infected lower intestine with a pro sports team owner?

☞ A flaming asshole.

☹ ☹ ☹

Sports team owners are men of their word....

☞ Just be sure you get it in writing.

☹ ☹ ☹

What's the difference between a Wall Street broker and a vulture?

☞ Vultures don't get Christmas bonuses.

☹ ☹ ☹

Did you hear about the Wall Street orgy?

☞ There was a rash of insider trading.

☹ ☹ ☹

How do you refer to a stockbroker who's always right?

☞ About to be indicted.

☹ ☹ ☹

What's a tryst for the typical Savings & Loan officer?

☞ The banker's thrust.

☹ ☹ ☹

When the wealthy Wall St. takeover specialist arrived to visit his new company he discovered an extraordinary number of well-endowed secretaries. Licking his lips, he turned to his assistant and said, "I'm staying around and exercising my stacked options. Call me in a week."

☹ ☹ ☹

Did you hear about the gay Savings & Loan officer?

☞ He was a real sperm banker.

☹ ☹ ☹

What do you call an impotent computer operator?

☞ A Floppy Dick.

LITERARY ACHIEVEMENTS: GRUNGE STYLE

☹ ☹ ☹

What are the world's most boring books?

The Secret Life of Accountants

The Models' Guide To The SAT & GRE Exams

Wall Street Brokers Who Made A Difference To Society

The Lawyers Handbook To Charitable Giving

☹ ☹ ☹

What are the world's most useless books?

The Iraqi Army Handbook On Military Tactics

The Anorexics' Guide To Giving Good Head

The Vegetarians' Guide To Blow-Job Substitutes

The Israeli Book Of Proper Etiquette

Low Cholesterol Soul Food

The Immigrants' Guide To Good Manners

The Arab Terrorist Handbook For Blowing Up Building And Not Getting Caught

☹ ☹ ☹

What are the world's most important books?

How To Say "No" When Your Clergyman Wants You To Say "Yes"
(New, Updated Gay and Straight Editions) ,

The Guide To Profits With Your Lying Stock Broker,

The Handbook For Dealing With Your Criminal Lawyer
(plus the yearly update: *Your Lawyer The Criminal*),

Nymphomania: How To Spread It,

The Guys' Guide To Good, Easy Girls Who Go Down,

The Woman's Guide To Improving Their Head,

The Low Budget Dating Book
(previously titled: *Masturbation My Way*),

Pee Wee Herman's Advice For Dealing

With Misdemeanor Charges: How To Get Yourself Off Without A Lawyer

Michael Jackson's Guide To Disappearing

☹ ☹ ☹

What did the hooker say at the computer programmers party?

☞ "This Wang's on me."

☹ ☹ ☹

What's a high tech prostitute?

☞ A portable lap-top.

☹ ☹ ☹

Why are airplane pilots who undergo frequent urine tests so irritable?

☞ They're constantly pissed off.

☹ ☹ ☹

What does a stewardess discreetly ask the male passengers she's interested in Fucking?

☞ Coffee, Tea or me?

☹ ☹ ☹

Why are airplane pilots on amphetamines so dangerous?

☞ When they crash, they take everybody with them.

☹ ☹ ☹

What's the best advice for a professional stripper?

☞ "Grin and bare it."

☹ ☹ ☹

What do you call a stewardess with V.D.?

☞ Aircraft carrier.

☹ ☹ ☹

Why should politicians have mistresses that fuck their brains out?

So they'll stop screwing us.

☹ ☹ ☹

What's a synonym for corrupt?

☞ Elected.

☹ ☹ ☹

What's an even better synonym for corrupt?

☞ Politician.

☹ ☹ ☹

And then, what is the true definition of corrupt?

☞ Republican.

☹ ☹ ☹

What's more unscrupulous than a politician?

☞ Two fuckin politicians.

☹ ☹ ☹

What can a politician break without touching?

☞ Campaign promises.

☹ ☹ ☹

What do you get when River Phoenix falls into a lettuce patch?

☞ Seizure salad.

CHAPTER SEVEN

GET RICH QUICK WITH RELIGION

Why are so many priests gay?

☞ They literally believe, "One good turn deserves another."

☹ ☹ ☹

Did you hear about the gay priest?

☞ He was so observant that every night he "Turned the other cheek."

☹ ☹ ☹

What is the holy sacrament for promiscuous Catholic priests?

☞ Little boys.

☹ ☹ ☹

What's sex education for Evangelical Christian, Catholic, Born Again and Orthodox Jewish school children?

☞ When the teachers take them to the zoo and the monkeys are fucking.

☹ ☹ ☹

What's a cross to a promiscuous nun?

☞ A phallic symbol.

☹ ☹ ☹

What's black and white and moans?

☞ A nun enjoying sex!

☹ ☹ ☹

What does the Happy Hooker have in common with the Virgin Mary?

☞ Both rode to glory on a little ass.

☹ ☹ ☹

How do we know that the Ten Commandments apply in the modern world?

☞ Because there are no Commandments against drugs and blowjobs.

What's an inflamed pussy for an observant Jew?

☞ The Burning Bush.

What's a TV Evangelist's holiest book?

☞ His Pocket Book, you fool.

Why can you Never trust TV Evangelists,

☞ They're all Fundamentally dishonest.

☹ ☹ ☹

Did you hear about the Fundamentalist who loved Hide & Seek?

☞ Every night he told his wife:
"Ready or not here I cum."

☹ ☹ ☹

What's water to a Buddhist monk?

☞ Fast food.

☹ ☹ ☹

Three Buddhist monks had been living in a mountain retreat for four years when one of them finally spoke.

"That was a fine pair of Tits that passed by the Monastery."

Three years go by. One of the other monks speaks up.

"She really was a great piece of ass."

Five more years pass. The third Buddhist can't take anymore and blurts out, "If you two keep up this bickering, I'm getting the fuck outa here!"

☹ ☹ ☹

During a flood, a Born Again takes refuge on his roof. The flood waters rise. Two men in a boat call out to him to jump aboard.

"No," he yells out. The Lord will take care of me."

Another boat offers help.

"No, the Lord will watch out for me."

Then a helicopter drops a line.

He waves it away. "The Lord will look after me."

He soon drowns and ascends to the Gates of Heaven. He angrily asks St. Peter why the Lord didn't look after him.

"What the Hell are you talking about you dumb shit? St. Peter says. "He sent you two God damned boats and a helicopter."

CHAPTER EIGHT

STAY SINGLE

How do you compute the true total American divorce rate?

☞ Take the number of marriages and divide by one.

☹ ☹ ☹

What did the right winger say to his bride on their wedding night?

☞ Love it or leave it! (Yeah, Bitch!)

☹ ☹ ☹

How can marrieds be certain to improve their sex life?

☞ Cheat.

☹ ☹ ☹

What's much worse than marrying a bad girl?

☞ Marrying a good one.

☹ ☹ ☹

Seattle Sal says: The cooing ends with the honeymoon...but the billing goes on forever.

☹ ☹ ☹

What savvy advice did the minister give the prospective redneck, white trash groom?

☞ Reach for the sty, partner.

☹ ☹ ☹

Seattle Sal says: The trend in modern matrimony is to shorter marriages...but more of 'em.

☹ ☹ ☹

What are the best grounds for divorce?

☞ Wherever you're standing.

☹ ☹ ☹

A woman went to a marriage counselor and said, "My husband isn't fit to live with the dogs."

"Don't be so negative," the counselor says. "Emphasize the positive."

"Okay, my husband is fit to live with the dogs."

☹ ☹ ☹

An old man marries a young bride. At the wedding, his best man asks him, "At your age aren't you worried about sex with such a young, pretty thing?"

He thinks about it for a moment. "Well," he says, "if she dies, she dies."

☹ ☹ ☹

Why is bigamy the only self-punishing crime?

☞ Because after you've committed it you've got two mother-in-laws.

☹ ☹ ☹

Two old men were talking about their old buddies who had died. "Of all of them I miss Johnny Day the most," one said.

"Why's that?"

"I married his widow."

☹ ☹ ☹

Two drunks were talking in a bar. "God," said one, "it's only been a week since my best friend ran off with my wife."

"Geez," said his companion, "You must feel terrible."

"Yeah," answered the down in the dumps fellow. "I miss him all ready."

☹ ☹ ☹

The relatives of a nervous virgin buy a pink negligee for her wedding night. She's to marry the good looking but also nervous son of the town's richest man.

When they checked it out at home, her relatives begin to worry that the gown was much too conservative so they tried to help things along by making it sexier. First her sister alters it, then the aunt hems it some more, and finally her mother also adjusts it.

On their wedding night, the nervous husband goes into the bathroom and undresses. Then he calls out to his new wife that he's ready. He'll be naked, he tells her, but she shouldn't look at him.

She remembers the pink negligee and hurries to unwrap it. Just as she opens it, he steps out of the bathroom. Looking inside the box, she says, "Oh my goodness what's that pink shriveled up little thing?"

"I told you not to look," he screams!

☹ ☹ ☹

Did you hear about the nervous virgin whose mother told her not to hold anything back on her wedding night?

☞ When her husband started to undress her, she shit in her dress.

☹ ☹ ☹

What are the two most frivolous words in the English language?

☞ "I do."

☹ ☹ ☹

What is the number one cause of divorce in North America?

☞ Marriage.

SEATTLE SAL'S "RELATIONSHIP SENSITIVITY TEST"

THE TEST:

☹ ☹ ☹

There is only one emotionally sensitive answer per question. Don't try to guess what it is. Just answer all questions honestly, then check the handy Answer Section in the back.

Congratulations! You've taken the first step on the road to a fuller, better, hipper, hotter, more sexually active relationship.

1. Imagine that a woman has purchased a smashing outfit that shows off her new, five pounds-lighter-than-last-week-figure. She and

her man go out dancing...and she turns every head in the place. Back home — finally! — and she slips into that special blue silk camisole. What might a sensitive man say:

A. "Boy am I beat."

B. "All right! The Sonics are on the tube tonight."

C. "Feel like a pizza?"

D. "On her best day Kathleen Turner never looked so fuckable!"

☹ ☹ ☹

2. In the dim candlelight of a favored French restaurant a couple share a quiet toast. This is exactly the right time to:

A. Joke about the blobs of sauce dripping down your lover's new silk blouse.

B. Comment sexually about the cheap blond or studly well-hung hunk at the next table.

C. Pull at the annoying strand of dental floss between your molars.

D. Propose while deeply massaging her thighs and then her breasts.

☹ ☹ ☹

3. After USING THE FACILITIES men should always put the toilet seat back down and flush! (In the event they forget to do so, they should feign profound remorse when said lapse is pointed out).

4. When a woman returns from the hairdresser with a bold new look a thoughtful man might say:

A. "Whaddya mean you forgot the beer Bitch?"

B. "The fuckin' VCR's on the fritz again."

C. "Honey could you wash the dishes?"

D. "Wow that's one terrific hairstyle. You now make me as hot and hard as I get while looking at the Penthouse Magazine pet pictures!"

☹ ☹ ☹

6. When a man models a boss new suit that makes him look hardcore and sexy to the max, a sensitive woman might say:

A. "We could both stand to lose a couple of pounds."

B. "What in the world could you have been thinking when you bought that pimp outfit?"

C. "Who died?"

D. "Come here Big Boy... I want to do you, right now!"

7. A couple arrive at a neighbor's barbecue and the man heads directly for the swimming pool. Forty five minutes later he still hasn't returned. When hunted down he's

found animatedly talking to a teenage girl bursting out of a bikini so tiny it would get her arrested in many Southern states. Later he might say to his disgusted girlfriend:

A. "Jenny's amazingly mature for sixteen."

B. "So you think the AFTA agreement was really a good idea?"

C. "I can't remember when I've felt more romantic."

D. "Honest, I'll never look at another teenager again if it upsets you.

☹ ☹ ☹

8. In a relationship which subject area is the least dangerous?

A. Pre-nuptual agreements.

B. Ex-lovers.

C. Orgasm.

D. Take out food.

☹ ☹ ☹

9. A couple is having a healthy, spirited conversation. (Argument is a pejorative, negative word that has outlived its usefulness). When the woman makes a pointed, yet perfectly legitimate, on-target remark how might a modern man conceivably respond?

A. "Are you getting your period?"

B. "I never laid a hand on that bitch, slut, dirtbag."

C. "You want me, I'll be with at the disco all night."

D. "Thanks for straightening me out. I certainly was wrong, I'm sorry."

☹ ☹ ☹

10. Two lovers are having cocktails before dinner. The woman, a tad tipsy, might make the following remark:

A. "So, how's Harry doing?" (The man's brother's name is Herb.).

B. "Thinning grey hair can look attractive. Really."

C. "Have we made love this month?"

D. "You make me so very happy, I'm gonna prove it to you tonight, honey!"

☹ ☹ ☹

11. What should a modern man-who-eschews-gender-stereotypes do when it's his turn to cook?

A. Complain and squeal like a stuck pig.

B. Slug down four double martinis before dinner.

C. Serve hamburger soup, as best you know how.

D. Buy a cookbook, take the day off and make a few different meals. Serving whichever one comes out best.

E. Get cracking on that Tex-Mex Radicchio and Lizard dish from the latest issue of GOURMET.

☹ ☹ ☹

12. When the subject of a man's salary comes up which of the following responses might a sensitive woman make?

A. "You call that a salary? I made more than that right out of college!"

B. "Alice and Phil have a house at Aspen this year. Again."

C "Thank God Daddy isn't alive."

D. "I'm so proud of you respect you for working so hard for your money. You are a man's man. You are my Man!"

☹ ☹ ☹

13. A woman's college roommate arrives for a long overdue visit. What should her mate do?

A. Make amusing comments about the breast enlargement surgery she has had.

B. Ask whether she's still concerned about the fuckin snail darter's safety.

C. Put the Red Hot Chil Peppers on the stereo. Loud.

D. Serve them snacks and drinks while listening attentively to the girls discussion of college guys they've both fucked.

☹ ☹ ☹

14. True or false? Even though he/she buys them gifts at Christmas and attends their birthday parties you secretly suspect

that your husband/wife wishes the kids had never been born.

TEST SCORING:

Award one point for every emotionally sensitive answer.

Answers: 1.D; 2.D; 3.Yes; 4.D; 5.C; 6.D; 7.D; 8.D; 9.D; 10.D;

11.D; 12.D; 13.D; 14.False!

WHAT YOUR SCORE MEANS

14 points:

A one in a million mate. (Are you, like, absolutely positive that you've answered all questions honestly?)

11-13 points:

About normal for the self-absorbed Americans of 1994. Distressing, but not hopeless. Work is required. (Call QFMC, Quick Fix Marriage Counseling.)

8-10 points:

Catastrophe. Massive psychotherapy needed. Situation grave. (Contact STEP, Shock Therapy and Erotic Paraphernalia, Inc.)

5-7 points:

Bad things so happen to good people. (Contact Columbus & Columbus & Rubin for a quick, cheap divorce.)

Below 5 points:

Get in your car and drive far away. When you get there, change your name. You are an asshole who doesn't deserve a good relationship. Go fuck yourself, as Al Goldstein of Screw Magazine would say.

COLLEGE GRUNGE

What Are The Top 10 Pressing Social Issues For American College Kids?

10. Tight Clothes: Around the crotch, chest or both.
9. Flannel Shirts
8. Sneakers: What brand to compliment one's personality?
7. Rings In Noses: To do or not to do?
6. Proper Diet: Veggie vs non-meat (exceptions allowed for girls on hot dates)?
5. Proper Morals: One sex partner vs multiple partners (per day)?
4. The Condom: who wears it, the man or the woman?
3. Sex Policy: Only with the one you love vs the one you can afford?

2. The Pill: The before pill vs the morning after pill?

1. View On Beavis and Butt-Head: Are they cool or do they suck?

☹ ☹ ☹

Why are America's college kids so health conscious?

☞ That's their justification for taking lots of pills and sticking needles in their arms.

CHAPTER NINE

RAW, CHAFING SEX

What did the masochistic flasher say to the cabbie?

☞ Step on it.

☹ ☹ ☹

Then there was the lonely cowboy who came back from a cattle drive a little steer crazy.

SEATTLE SAL'S PATHETIC PUNS

☹ ☹ ☹

Why was the rich wife proud to give birth to the Mexican gardener's child?

☞ It was the first Manuel labor she'd ever done.

☹ ☹ ☹

What did the shocked husband say when his wife suddenly plunged into his lap and chewed his penis?

☞ "That was a gnaw-ful thing to do."

☹ ☹ ☹

Why did the frog cover his bride with mud in their wedding night?

☞ Slime was of the essence.

☹ ☹ ☹

What did the shy, nervous, guy say to his hot date while eating Italian food?

☞ Er, Uh, By the way, are you pro-valone or anti-pasta?

GRUNGEY WORD GAMES

☹ ☹ ☹

What does L.S.D. really stand for?

☞ Losers Sell Drugs, Let's Self Destruct or Let's Suck Dicks (take your choice, dudes).

☹ ☹ ☹

What does C.I.A. really stand for?

☞ Cocaine In America.

☹ ☹ ☹

JOCKS, An acronym for....

Jerks (with)
Offensive
Cocks (who)
Keep
Sucking

☹ ☹ ☹

ISRAEL, An acronym for....

I
Should
Receive
An
Easy
Life

☹ ☹ ☹

IRAQIS, An acronym for....

I

Ran

Ans

Quit

I'm

Smart

☹ ☹ ☹

IRANIAN, An acronym for....

I'll

Run

And

Nap

I

Ain't

Nut

MORE DUMB PUNS

☹ ☹ ☹

What do you call an affair between a boring couple and another boring man?

☞ A "menage a blah."

☹ ☹ ☹

What's the difference between meat and fish?

☞ It's no fun to beat your fish.

AND EVEN MORE OF SAL'S STUPID PUNS

☹ ☹ ☹

Why did the virgin sleep with the tycoon?

☞ He had a yacht to offer.

☹ ☹ ☹

How's a homely girl like a bank account.

☞ Both draw almost no interest.

☹ ☹ ☹

One evening a man spots a good-looking nun on a bus. When she gets off, he asks the bus driver smiles and replies about her.

"Oh, Sister Mary rides this line for daily Vespers at the cemetery."

At dusk the next evening, the man goes to the cemetery, and once there dresses up as Jesus.

When the nun arrives, he steps out from behind a grave marker and says, "I am Jesus Christ. I want to fuck you in the ass."

"Yes, Oh Lord," the nun replies gleefully, and bends over.

Delighted, the man lifts up her habit and begins to defile the sister. After climaxing, he rips off his beard and says, "I'm not really Jesus Christ."

The nun rips off her habit. "And I'm not really the nun. I'm the gay bus driver."

☹ ☹ ☹

A woman goes to a doctor. During the examination, he notices one tit is two inches longer than another. "When did this start happening?" he asks, concerned.

"Since my husband started sucking every night," she tells him.

"That shouldn't do it," the confused doctor says, "Something isn't right."

"Well we sleep in bunk beds."

☹ ☹ ☹

A man with a huge swollen cock is in the hospital. A fly lands on its tip. "Nurse, nurse," he calls out. "That fly is bothering me."

The nurse holds the dick and goes to swat the fly, but can't reach it as it quickly moves around to the other side of the infected member. She grabs the Cock again and this time tries to brush it off.

"Oops, it flew away," she says.

"That's all right," the man assures her. "If

you keep doing that, I'll plaster the little bastard to the ceiling."

☹ ☹ ☹

How were Tarzan and Jane a modern couple?

☞ They both wanted to swing.

☹ ☹ ☹

Who comes from an exotic place and likes to hang around playgrounds and look up girls' dresses?

☞ Jungle Jim.

☹ ☹ ☹

Why was the nympho disappointed in the Navy?

☞ She found out the nineteen inch Admiral was just a television set.

☹ ☹ ☹

What's bad news for the Dairy Queen?

☞ Sex with Mr. Softee.

"PERSONALS IN THE *SEATTLE*
FAVORITE PERSONAL ADS

LIGHT MY FIRE

Straight SM great personality, hot body, w/ burns over 60% of body, searching for sensible relationship. Poor eyesight a must, easy morals a plus.

HANDS OFF THE HAIR

Bored WF in 40's, blond, lwyr, seeks younger man for discreet, active SXL affair. Pvt. jet, large white house in central. D.C. location, Must have own whips and chains. (Husb. pub. fig. who travels alot).

INTO BONDAGE:

Desperate SWM hostage seeks hrny wman for intimate SXL relationship. Libido vs. strong. Beirut vicinity.

Open-Minded Parents Wntd
SWM seeks wh. or bk. young boy for fun. Enjoy Lit. League, mrbles, war gmes. (Micheal Jackson style) Ice cream guarntd. Discretn a must. (Nap time obsrvd).

WIDE RECEIVER:
SWF seeks high scring ftball team that knows all the right MVS. No cleats. I am ready for action, ready to go down.

NEARLY NORMAL:
SWM sks SWM or SWF into tuba sex, sports gear, rubber soldiers, S & M, bottles, hamsters and sewing paraphnlia. No weirdos, please.

LOVE ME I'M A LIBERAL
Sngle W. Fem. seeks Black Male, Any species, w/ bg ck, for wild & drty sex 3x/day or don't reply. Into bndge & humiliation. Non-smoking. Cath. preferred.

FAIRY TAIL:
Ms. Tuffet type seeks SWM to sit on muffet and face. Send photo, tongue size, ck lengt., specific sex desires. Hurry, I'm hrny.

VOLT FOR ME:
Mad Scientist seeks striking beauty w/bg tits for srious rltinship, hrny hot sx,
& weird SXL expermnts. Elctrfyng personaly. AC/DC ok. Dsre for crly hair helpfl.

MS. BOTTOM LINE:
Pragmatic nympho ready to settle down w/ Mr. Right. Send Photo, Bank Balnce, Penis Length & Thickness (whn stff).# times you cum & othr rlvnt dtails.

MISOGYNIST:
Sx mchine type seeks lovng sexual rltnship w/submisve sxly prmsiv, Female-type wman or any sub-species. I'm rdy, wiling, adn able (and hrny).

CHEVY AVAILABLE

Chicano real macho man w/ grn card and muy grande cock, seeks SWF Coll. Grad. Blonde with big tits, big ass, big lips & jumpr cables. Satisfaction grntd.

CHAPTER TEN

BEAVIS AND BUTT-HEAD'S GUIDE TO SAFE SEX

Why should we all be thankful that Beavis and Butt-Head jerk off so much?

☞ It's a dirty job and someone has to do it.

☹ ☹ ☹

What's walking masturbation for Beavis and Butt-Head?

☞ A pocketful of miracles (or instant gratification).

☹ ☹ ☹

Why are Beavis and Butt-Head so into masturbation?

1) They believe in practicing Safe Sex.
2) They feel the end justifies the means.
3) They beleive in having sex only with someone they really love.

☹ ☹ ☹

What excuse did Beavis come up with when his mother caught him masturbating?

☞ Extenuating circumstances.

☹ ☹ ☹

What excuse did Butt-Head come up with when he was caught?

☞ "Dating and girls cost a lot a money these days...heh, heh, heh!".

☹ ☹ ☹

Why are Beavis and Butt-Head considered by their girlfriends to be sexually incompetent?

☞ Because they're premature ejerkulators.

☹ ☹ ☹

What happened to Beavis when he had an erection and walked into a wall?

☞ He hurt his nose.

SAFE SEX NERD STYLE

"My girl friend is incredibly considerate," said the nerd to his friend, "always thinking of others."

"Yeah how?"

"She brings another guy on all our dates."

"What?"

"Yep. That way only one of us goes home depressed."

☹ ☹ ☹

How did the virgin nerd try to avoid sex?

☞ He tried to fight off his left hand while his right hand pumped.

☹ ☹ ☹

How did Butt-Head attempt to stop jerking off?

☞ By trying to restrain his right hand while the left one was beating his meat.(or choking-his-chicken or strangling-his-snake or spanking-his-monkey or jerkin'-the-gerkin, or...)

P.S. Readers, if you've got ay other cool expressions that are variations on this, please send them to me for inclusion in the next book I do. I'll put your name in the book as a thank you if I use your expressions.

And as a reward, I'll send you a copy of my last book GRUNGE JOKES ($4.99 retail price) for free! The only catch is that I've got to ask you to send in $3.00 for shipping and handling. The address to send your suggested jokes, your money and your address to receive your complimentary book is:

S.P.I. Books
136 West 22nd St.
New York, NY 10011

You can send check, money order or cash made out to S.P.I. Books).

☹ ☹ ☹

What's two-handed masturbation for Beavis and Butt-Head?

☞ A menage a trois.

☹ ☹ ☹

What do you call a young nerd?

☞ An immature ejerkulator.

☹ ☹ ☹

Nerds sure are confused. They play the skin flute... to make their organs sing.

☹ ☹ ☹

Who plays second fiddle for a nerd?

☞ The left hand.

☹ ☹ ☹

What's Beavis and Butt-Head's favorite sport?

☞ Pocket pool.

☹ ☹ ☹

Who did the Mayor of L.A. blame the recent Los Angeles fires on?

☞ "We're sure Beavis and Butt-Head did it."

☹ ☹ ☹

If you had a machine gun and were in a room with Jeffrey Dahmer, Adolph Hitler, Joey Buttufuocco and Beavis and Butt-Head–what do you do?

☞ Empty the clip into Beavis and Butt-Head–They're definitely more damaging to millions of young kids who watch them each day!

CHAPTER ELEVEN

MORONS FOREVER

Why did the moron mutilate himself in the stereo shop?

☞ Because he was told everything there costs an arm and a leg.

☹ ☹ ☹

A moron sitting at one end of a bar tells the bartender to serve a drink on him to a woman sitting at the other end. "You don't want to do that," the bartender says.

"Yes, I do," the moron insists. The bartender shrugs and serves her a shot. She gulps it down, but doesn't even look up.

"Give her another one on me," the moron instructs him.

"Don't waste your money," the bartender argues. But the moron again insists. So the bartender serves up a second drink and again the woman gulps it down and doesn't even look the moron's way.

The moron tries a third time. "Look," the bartender confides, "you don't want to do that. She's a fucking Lesbian."

"Give her another," the moron insists. Just after the bartender pours the woman a third drink, the moron approaches her.

"Hi," he says, "My name's Mortimer. What part of Lesbia are you from?"

☹ ☹ ☹

Did you hear about the moron who went to the beach to meet women. A guy told him they were all at the Sand Bar. So he swam out there and could'nt find any babes...The place must have been closed.

☹ ☹ ☹

What do you get when you combine a moron with Benito Mussolini?

☞ Il Dunce.

☹ ☹ ☹

Why did the moron shoot his Wheaties?

☞ He wanted to be a cereal killer.

☹ ☹ ☹

Why did the moron think his wife loved baseball?

☞ Every time she passed a jewelry shop she got pendant fever.

☹ ☹ ☹

Why did the moron try to fuck his girlfriend in the ear?

☞ He wanted to try some aural sex.

☹ ☹ ☹

One old moron turned to a group of his buddies and said loudly, "Windy, ain't it?"

"No, it ain't," shouted back one of the old timers whose hearing aide batteries were low. "It's Thursday."

"Me too!" yelled a third geezer, "Let's get a drink."

☹ ☹ ☹

Why did the moron jump out of the airplane?

☞ A friend told him to air is human.

☹ ☹ ☹

Why did the moron join the Navy?

☞ He wanted to be active in sperm warfare...against the WACs.

☹ ☹ ☹

Why did the moron expose himself in church?

☞ He said he wanted to be a Moonie.

☹ ☹ ☹

Why did the moron refuse to be a Jehovah's Witness?

☞ He said he didn't even see the damn accident.

☹ ☹ ☹

Why did the moron pray in front of the deli?

☞ Hero worship.

☹ ☹ ☹

Why did the moron's discount massage parlor fail?

☞ It was self-service.

☹ ☹ ☹

Why did the moron bring a ladder to the party?

☞ He heard the drinks were on the house.

☹ ☹ ☹

What did the moron say to the boy whose left hand was cut off in an accident?

☞ "Don't worry, you'll be all right."

☹ ☹ ☹

A moron walking down the street was dressed in full pirate regalia, including wooden sword, cocked hat and eye patch.

"What are you supposed to be?" asked a passing woman.

"A pirate. Whatta ya think lady?"

"Well if you're a pirate where are your buccaneers?"

"Under my buckin' hat dumb bitch," growled the moron.

☹ ☹ ☹

Why did the moron woman have so much trouble using birth control pills?

☞ Every time she stood up, they fell out.

CHAPTER TWELVE

ANIMALS, DEAD OR ALIVE

☹ ☹ ☹

What's it called when a vampire cuts in line at the blood bank?

☞ Batting out of turn.

☹ ☹ ☹

What do you call a dumb silent kitty?

☞ Catatonic.

☹ ☹ ☹

What's tan and white and rapes dogs?

☞ Lassie the Nympho.

☹ ☹ ☹

What's green and red and goes three hundred miles an hour?

☞ Kermit...in a blender.

☹ ☹ ☹

A confused drunk is talking to a bartender.

"Hey do lemons have wings?"

"Of course not!"

"Well, then I just squeezed your fuckin canary into my drink."

☹ ☹ ☹

Why do dogs lick their balls constantly?

☞ Because they can.

☹ ☹ ☹

What do you call a cat with only three lives?

☞ An Iraqi.

☹ ☹ ☹

What do you get when you cross a steamroller with a poodle?

☞ A puddle.

☹ ☹ ☹

What stinks has four legs and flies?

☞ A dead horse.

☹ ☹ ☹

What did the elephant say to the naked man?

☞ It's cute...but can you pick up peanuts with it.

☹ ☹ ☹

What is the most important thing to remember about sex with an elephant?

☞ Always stay on top.

☹ ☹ ☹

A female elephant had a thorn in her foot. She saw a passing ant and said, "If you take this thorn out, I'll let you fuck me."

"Oh boy," said the horny ant, who busily went to work on the thorn. With a mighty pull for such a little guy, it came out. "Now I get to fuck you," the ant proudly stated.

He climbed up the side of the elephant and worked his way to the her ample Pussy. "Ready?" he shouted as he stuck it in as deeply as he could.

"Go ahead," the elephant replied, while giggling and not feeling a thing "Take me, I'm yours!"

As the ant was humping away with all his might, a monkey in a tree above dropped a coconut onto the elephant's head. The elephant shrieked, "Ow!"

"That's right!" the ant yelled in ecstasy, "Take it all, bitch."

☹ ☹ ☹

What's grey and cums in quarts?

☞ A horny elephant.

☹ ☹ ☹

How do you know if an elephant's been fucking your wife?

☞ The definitive sign is grey hide under her fingernails.

☹ ☹ ☹

A nymphomaniac decides to have sex with three little virgin male pigs. The first pig, on hearing that she's coming to fuck him, wraps his cock with straw. When the nympho sees this, she says, "I'll huff and I'll puff and I'll blow your cock off." At the end of the session, he no longer has a cock or even his balls left.

The second pig thinks he'll be smarter and builds a wooden box around his cock. On seeing the makeshift chastity belt, the nympho says, "I'll huff and I'll puff and I'll blow your cock off." She goes to work and sucks his manhood to splinters.

The third pig decides to take no chances and covers his cock with cement. It hardens just before the nympho gets there. "I'll huff and I'll puff and I'll blow your cock off," she says while beginning to go down on him.

She looks up again in sudden delight. "Just what I like in a pig," she says, "A cock that's hard as a rock."

☹ ☹ ☹

A farmer and his wife return home to a grisly scene. In the barnyard they find all their chickens dead from cruel and violent mutilation of their sexual organs. They move along to find a dead pig, a dead mare, and a dead cow in succession, all similarly damaged and defiled.

They go around behind the barn and spot their prize rooster unscathed and smiling while lying in the shade. The farmer realizes the rooster was the horny culprit and bends down to pick it up.

The rooster opens one eye, shushes, him, and points to the vultures circling overhead.

☹ ☹ ☹

What do you get when you mate a hooker and a deer?

☞ A horny bitch who fucks for bucks.

☹ ☹ ☹

What is silent and smells like worms?

☞ A bird fart.

☹ ☹ ☹

Did you hear why W.C. Fields wouldn't drink water?

☞ "Fish fuck in the stuff."

☹ ☹ ☹

Did you hear about the skunk who declared bankruptcy because he was scent-less?

☹ ☹ ☹

What's got whiskers and scratches at glass?

☞ Garfield in the microwave.

☹ ☹ ☹

What do you call it when an alligator sucks your cock?

☞ Gone.

☹ ☹ ☹

Why is it so difficult to smell moth balls?

☞ It's hard getting their little legs apart.

☹ ☹ ☹

What's green and wrinkled and smells like Miss Piggy?

☞ Kermit's finger.

☹ ☹ ☹

Why did Minnie Mouse leave Mickey Mouse?

☞ She was tired of the same old rat race.

☹ ☹ ☹

How do we know that the shark attack victim had dandruff?

☞ His head and shoulders washed up on the beach.

☹ ☹ ☹

What's the last thing that goes through an insect's brain when it hits your windshield?

☞ Its asshole.

IN HONOR OF PRESIDENT BILL CLINTON: CHICKEN JOKES.

Why did the pretty chicken run away from the moron rooster?

☞ He called her foxy.

☹ ☹ ☹

What are the two scariest movies that chickens all over the world are afraid of?

☞ *The Right Stuffing* and *Five Easy Pieces.*

☹ ☹ ☹

What should a teenage rooster never do?

☞ Come home stewed after fucking like a bird.

☹ ☹ ☹

What do chickens always get when they buy new cars?

☞ Hatchbacks.

CHAPTER THIRTEEN

JUST PLAIN GRUNGEY

SEATTLE SAL'S "PHILOSOPHICAL PONDERING" #1:

If you want to impress the babes with how deep and smart you are, then study these sure-fire, Sure-to-get-you-laid-questions, and use them on the next girl whose pants you'd like to get into!

1.Why is it that bodily excrements from other people — shit, piss, vomit, snot, etc. — should disgust us so much when we all carry them around inside us?

2. What do you think, honey? is a person's beautiful hair so lovely until...it's in your butter. Did you ever think about that, dear?

3. What do you think about premeditated oral sex where we both take a shower so we taste better? Wouldn't that be an improvement, darling?

☹ ☹ ☹

What did the high school teacher say after she fucked one of her students?

☞ I'll see you right after my next period.

☹ ☹ ☹

Why is anal sex like a long trip?

☞ Because you start up a dark avenue, then proceed along a dusty street, onto a dirt road, all to get to the Hershey Highway.

☹ ☹ ☹

What did the two horny girls say about the nude, sun bathing, well hung guy they spotted in the secluded area of the park?

☞ "Oh, he's a real snake in the grass."

☹ ☹ ☹

"Daddy, Daddy," said the boy, "What's a pervert?"

☞ "Shut up and keep sucking."

What electrical life-support system do fat people depend on?

☞ A refrigerator.

What do you get when you fuck at the beach with a sunburn?

☞ Sex a peel.

What's worse than finding out your blind date is ugly?

☞ Finding out your ugly date is also blind.

☹ ☹ ☹

How can you tell if your blind date is too fat?

☞ If when she sits on your face and you can't hear the stereo.

☹ ☹ ☹

Why was the nice blind man arrested for molesting children?

☞ He was trying to read their body language.

☹ ☹ ☹

Did you hear about the guy who lost his left testicle?

☞ He's all right now.

☹ ☹ ☹

What's the best thing to do if you find a strange epileptic in your swimming pool?

☞ Throw in your laundry.

☹ ☹ ☹

Why don't midget women like to use tampons?

☞ They keep tripping on the strings.

☹ ☹ ☹

How did the horny wife warm up dinner for her horny husband?

☞ She slid down a banister.

☹ ☹ ☹

What's dessert for a serious bulemic?

☞ Two fingers.

☹ ☹ ☹

A drunk walked into a bar late one evening and seeing that the only other customers in the place were a middle-aged couple at the far end, he decided to be generous.

"Give me a scotch and soda," he said, "and give that gentleman and that douche bag down there whatever they want."

The bartender gave the drunk a steely glare and asked. "What did you just say?"

The drunk, with a look of sublime innocence, repeated his request.

"I'd like a scotch and soda, and give that fellow and that douche bag with him anything they want."

"Wait a minute, pal!" erupted the barkeep. "Where do you get off coming into my place and insulting my customers? They're human beings, entitled to dignity and respect. I won't tolerate your appalling behavior in my establishment." He paused and took a deep breath. "I'll ask you once more, what I can do for you, and I'd better not hear what I just heard!"

"You're absolutely right," said the drunk. "Excuse me, I was out of line. Give me a scotch and soda, and please give that gentleman and that lady with him whatever they want."

"Now you're talking," said the smiling bartender. He ambled down to the couple at the far end. "Pardon me folks. But that gentleman would like to buy you both a drink."

"That's very nice," answered the man. "I'll have a vodka martini, shaken not stirred."

"And you madam?" asked the barman.

The woman smiled. "I'll have a vinegar and water."

SEATTLE SAL'S "MATHEMATICAL WORD PROBLEMS":

☹ ☹ ☹

Problem #1: When making out with your date in the back seat of your friend's car, while he's driving at 35 mph, and you French kiss her for five minutes, pet her for seven minutes, finger her for two, go down on her for two more, then get sucked off for six, exactly how far have you traveled during your make-out session?

☞ Answer: Around the world.

☹ ☹ ☹

Problem # 2: How much does it cost to clean ten a thousand gallon septic tank with a hose two inches in diameter that can pump at one gallon per minute on a cost-to-time ratio of ten dollars per minute?

☞ Answer: A shitload.

☹ ☹ ☹

Problem #3: What's 2 plus 2 plus 2 plus 2 minus 1?

☞ Answer: A swinging couples' orgy after your angry uptight wife has left.

CHAPTER FOURTEEN

MISS AMERICA GRUNGE

How can you identify Miss Arkansas at the Miss America Beauty Pageant?

☞ She's the dumb one with tobacco juice dripping down her chin.

☹ ☹ ☹

How can you identify Miss New York at the Miss America Beauty Pageant?

☞ She's the aggressive one with cum dripping down her face!

☹ ☹ ☹

How can you identify Miss California at the Miss America Beauty Pageant?

☞ She's the fidgity one with coke powder residue around her nostrils.

☹ ☹ ☹

How can you identify Miss Puerto Rico at the Miss America Beauty Pageant?

☞ She's the nervous one with crack powder dripping out of her nose.

☹ ☹ ☹

How can you identify Miss Jamaica at the Miss America Beauty Pageant?

☞ She's the one so high on ganja that she's stumbling around the stage.

(Dear Reader, Do you know what is wrong with one of these Beauty Pageant questions which makes it an impossible and illogical question to answer? If you do know what's wrong and how Seattle Sal has tricked your ass, then send me a letter telling me what's wrong and I'll send you a copy of my previous best-selling joke book GRUNGE JOKES.

There's one catch, you've got to send me $3.00 (check, money order, or cash) to cover the costs of shipping and handling.

Also, send me a few of the funniest jokes you've heard and I'll put em in my next joke book and I'll give you name credit in the book! Thanks for your help, Seattle Sal.

P.S. I'll tell you what's wrong with the one joke because I know you are all too stupid to figure it out....*(The joke about Jamaica is impossible and illogical because they are not competitors in the Miss America Pageant–they're some other fucking banana republic country!)*

☹ ☹ ☹

How can you identify Miss Detroit at the Miss America Beauty Pageant?

☞ She's the one with the mace tucked in her sash.

☹ ☹ ☹

What do you get if you cross Cindy Crawford, Sharon Stone and an onion?

☞ A fantasy piece of ass so incredible it will make you cry.

The 1993-1994 GRUNGE Series:

Grunge Jokes

Grungier Jokes

Hard Core Grunge Jokes

Christmas Grunge Jokes